Complete Guide to Passing the UK Practical Driving Test

Henry Norsworthy

Published in 2024

Copyright © 2024

Henry Norsworthy

ISBN: 9798320844176

While all of the information in this book has come from official sources such as driving instructors and the DVLA and has been checked to assure it is up to date as of 2024, I am not a qualified driving instructor and so this book is just notes that I took before my test and are being shared as just what helped me to learn to drive properly and pass my test.

Contents

Ways to practice
One of the best ways to practice
is to use someone you knows car
with them supervising (they must
be at least 21 and held their
licence for three years) and using
learner insurance such as Veygo
learner insurance which can let
you select from as little as one
hour (three hours is £6), or RAC
learner insurance which is £16 for
24 hours and gets cheaper for
extended periods. Lessons with an
instructor cost an average of £32
an hour.

Car for the test
To take the test you do not need a
dual-control car and so you can

use your friends or family's car however if hiring a car then you will be required to hire a dual-control car. You will also need to buy a suction stick-on rear-view mirror for the examiner (can be bought on amazon for around £8). You can also hire your instructor's car if they offer that.

Booking a test

There is a large backlog of tests booked and so to book a test there must be a cancellation. Apps such as Testi will automatically send you a notification once a test slot becomes available which can be booked on a first come first serve basis. A test costs £62.

Test objective

The driving test is to see if when driving independently you can drive competently (control of the car, know the law and theory of the road etc.) and safely (sufficient awareness, planning, observations etc.). If the examiner has to interfere (grab the wheel, use dual control pedals, tell you to slow down, tell you that you have stalled etc.) or does not feel safe (non-appropriate speed for situation, lack of observations etc.) then the examiner will not think you are ready to be on the road yet and will not pass you on that occasion.

On the test

Examiner will ask —

- Read a cars registration from 20 meters
- One show me tell me question before test e.g., how do you check your lights are working, how do you check tyre pressure, how do you check oil level etc. (videos can be found on Youtube for the car you are using)
- Different types of driving - following the examiners sat-nav, following the examiners instructions, and independent driving following signs
- Along the way there will be multiple pull up when it's safe and pull away again with at least one being on a busy road

and one being parked close
behind a parked car

- One show me tell me question
during the test e.g., how do you
roll your window down, how
do you clean the front
windscreen, how do you demist
the rear window etc.

- Manoeuvre – can be; park
forward into a bay, reverse
park into a bay, parallel park
(most commonly will be on the
left side), or reverse back two
spaces

- Emergency stop – might not
be on your test but the
examiner will tell you that
you're doing the emergency
stop, for this you will be on a
quiet road and the examiner

will check if its safe first and will raise their hand and tell you to stop and you don't look before stopping just press the break as fast and as hard as you can then put the handbrake on and put the car in neutral (not reacting quick enough or not pressing the brake hard enough can result in a fail)

Faults

Examiner will record mistakes that you make on an iPad e.g., forget to check mirrors is a minor fault, running a red light is a serious fault etc.

- Three minor faults of same kind = fail
- 15 minor faults = fail
- One serious fault = fail

Driving

Pulling off (to the right)

- Seatbelt
- Start engine
- Press brake
- Handbrake off
- Lift clutch to bite (you will feel the car slightly tilt forward like it's trying to go)
- Pulling out to right with a car parked in front -
- Look over left shoulder to check left blind spot (area that is not able to be seen in mirrors)
- Left mirror
- Right mirror
- Dry steer to right

- Look over right shoulder to check right blind spot (failing to do so is a minor, if someone was coming it's a serious) (if something is coming and have to wait then check right blind spot again before moving)
- If it's clear gently accelerate while steering right and come off the clutch
- If on a hill don't take off the handbrake until last second and get the car at biting point and begin accelerating slightly before taking off the handbrake and once taken off handbrake accelerate a bit more than normal (rolling back can be a serious if there is something behind)
- If can't see down the road if there is something is coming

reverse back if possible while either looking over shoulder out the back window or in the center mirror to give larger window to see out of the front down the road, if in a tight space then edge out very slowly to alert oncoming traffic you intend to pull out which should cause them to stop then continue edging out slowly until the road is visible

- Once the front of the car is clear of the car in front start steering left
- Once driving, if there is no oncoming traffic, on residential roads drive in the middle of the road to give good distance from parked cars and have

good observation and therefore anticipation of what is ahead (planning and awareness) – if you can't see what is ahead (such as an uphill) or see past something (such as a bend or large parked vehicle) then slow right down and be prepared to take action if necessary and therefore avoid harsh braking if something does appear

Changing up gear/ increasing speed

- Revs at two/ can hear and feel gear change is necessary
- Center mirror (failing to check mirrors (observations) is a minor but serious if it causes you to miss information that leads to you driving

dangerously e.g., cutting someone up, causing someone to change speed, or if a car goes into the back of you etc.)

- Come off the accelerator and press the clutch down and change gear
- Ease off the clutch while starting to accelerate again
- Gears: below 10mph = first gear, 10mph – 25mph = second gear, 25mph – 35mph = third gear, 35mph – 50mph = fourth gear, 50mph – 70mph = fifth gear

Braking

- Slowing down; the car in front of you is braking (red lights on

the back of the car), see a red
light in the distance, a light that
has been green for a while and
is likely to change, can't see far
enough down the road ahead
etc.

- Center mirror
- Brake
- Change to a lower gear

Stopping

- Center mirror
- Brake
- Change to a lower gear
- Hold the clutch down when
  below 10mph
- Change into first gear
- If on a hill use the handbrake

Pulling off again

- Check left and right mirrors in case a bike is about to pull in front of you (minor but serious if there was a bike)
- If clear ahead or light has turned green and traffic is moving then once at around 10mph change to second gear

Stalling

- If the car jolts forward and stalls it's due to not accelerating enough and coming of the clutch too quickly. As lifting the clutch to biting point accelerate but as the car starts moving keep the clutch at biting point for a few seconds before coming off

- If stall then hold down both the brake and clutch
- Turn the key down then up to turn the car back on (if holding the clutch you don't need to put it back in neutral which will make pulling off faster to not hold up traffic behind and get beeped which can be a minor but it can be a serious if stall on a junction or on a roundabout and block the flow of traffic or cause traffic to take evasive action)
- Check all mirrors
- Pull away

Steering

- Always check center mirror
and the side mirror in the
direction you plan to steer
before steering (even a little
bit) because there could be a
bike trying to overtake (minor
but can be a serious if there is a
bike approaching)
- Keep hands in ten to two
positions
- Don't overlap hands when
steering - push and pull/ feed
the wheel hand to hand
keeping them at the ten to two
position

Signalling

- Always check center mirror and the side mirror in the direction you plan to turn before signalling (minor but can be a serious if someone is trying to overtake)

- When approaching a junction, if there is a turning before the junction in the direction you intend to turn, do not signal until after the turning because someone coming from that turning might think you are turning into that road and so think it's safe for them to pull out, this is a serious

- Same when pulling up, if there is a turning in the direction that you intend to pull up coming up don't start signalling until past the turning

- When pulling away, wait until there are no cars coming before signalling because your signal might encourage them to stop which would be a minor for stopping the flow of traffic, only signal when cars are coming if it is very busy and there is no break in the traffic and therefore would rely on someone letting you go

Clearance

- If there are cars parked on your side of the road, you would need to move into the lane for oncoming traffic, and therefore you must give way to oncoming traffic before you move into the oncoming lane (serious). If there is oncoming traffic when approaching the parked car check center mirror, slow down, come into second gear, check center and right mirror, and come into the center of the road more to have a good view ahead but leave good space for oncoming traffic to pass as well leave good distance/ don't get right up behind the car parked on your side and stop, this will allow you to see if any more cars are coming before going and won't have to turn sharply to pull out again. Vice versa if oncoming traffic had cars parked on their side then it is your priority and they must give way to you

- If it's clear when approaching
  cars parked on your side, check
  center mirror, slow down,
  come into second gear, and
  keep looking ahead to see if
  any oncoming cars appear, if
  it's clear check center and right
  mirror and if no bikes are
  overtaking use the road for
  oncoming traffic to continue.
  Once you have committed to
  passing the cars parked on your
  side, if any oncoming traffic
  appears they must let you finish

- Or when approaching cars
  parked on the left, even though
  there is oncoming traffic there
  could be enough room to go as
  well, check center mirror, slow
  down, and come into second

gear and whilst approaching. Judge if the gap is wide enough for you to go and if not sure slow right down and stop if necessary, if it seems wide enough then check center and right mirror and if no bike is overtaking go, when driving within a car doors length of parked cars on your left you should go no more than 5mph, if there is a bit more room then 10mph, bit more room then 15mph etc. (clearance) (in case a door opens or someone steps out - minor if too fast and serious if too close to the parked cars on the left and the examiner has to move the wheel right)

- If there are parked cars on both sides then whoever goes

first has the right of way, if
both go together at the same
time then whoever has a space
to pull into should pull into the
space to let traffic pass. If there
is no immediate space then
whoever has the least amount
of distance to reverse back to a
space should reverse back

- If steering around a bend or
turning into a new road when
there are parked cars don't just
go immediately into the road,
go slow and see if there is
traffic coming first because
otherwise you will just have to
reverse to let them come
through

Overtaking

- Make sure can see fully down the road ahead
- Signal right in good time before pulling out
- Check center and right mirror
- Only overtake if you can overtake without needing to exceed the speed limit, and if overtaking is allowed on the road you are on (double solid lines in the middle means no overtaking)
- Expect busses to be stopping so keep an eye on their indicators and hold back a bit more. When a stopped bus is pulling away and indicates right you must let it go
- Sometimes a car might be signalling left even though

there's no turning coming up
so hold back because they
might be approaching a space
that they intend to drive past
then reverse into, when they
reverse into the space the front
of their car is going to swing
out so don't try and overtake
and let them go into the space
then once they are in enough
and it doesn't look like they are
going to come back out to
correct then can continue. If
there is no oncoming traffic on
other side of the road and can
completely clear the left side of
the road then can signal right
and just go around without
waiting

Turning (right)

- Approaching turning check center and right-side mirrors
- Signal right
- Slow right down on approach and come into second gear and keep in your lane (can go in hatch-markings if they are there)
- Look for speed sign for the new road
- Drive up until the wing mirror is in line with the center of road you are turning into and look down the road to make sure it's clear further along and nothing is coming
- Stop if there is oncoming traffic and go into first gear and wait for a gap

- When it looks like it's going to be clear check center and right mirror

- Turn into road keeping within the left lane (serious if go in right lane). If there are cars parked immediately on the left on the road, still come into the road in the left lane then once in the road move into the right lane to go around the parked cars (although outside of a driving test this doesn't matter)

- If you are turning right and stop at a light, when the light turns green (a solid green light with no arrow) then this means proceed with caution and you can go forward to be parallel with your road and even if there a yellow box you can still go forward but if there is oncoming traffic on the other side of the road they have the right of way and you must stop and give way to the oncoming traffic then once they have gone by then finish the turn. If there is a green arrow (called a filter light) pointing in the direction you want to go which is usually located on the side or underneath the traffic light then this indicates that the oncoming traffic on the other side of the road have been given a red signal and it's your right of way to go but still look down the road before going in case there is an emergency services vehicle coming and you won't be able to make the

turn in time (again - solid green
light and turning right go
forward with caution and be
prepared to stop for oncoming
traffic before turning, green
right arrow you can go but still
check first) (when approaching
a light if there is a designated
area for cyclists at the front and
you stop in it then it is a
serious)
Filter light

Speed signs

- Sign when entering a new road
- Painted on the road
- In cities, towns, small residential areas, and areas with schools it is usually 20mph
- If there are lamp posts then that means 30mph unless stated otherwise
- There is a speed sign on every sixth lamp post from when entering a new road
- Big speed signs means that it has just changed to that speed/ it is the beginning of that speed zone (if you can see a speed sign for a road that turns off of the road you are on and it is a big speed sign then that indicates the road you are on has a different speed limit)

- Small speed signs are reminders
  of the speed limit in the zone
  you are already in

- National speed limit (white
  circle with diagonal black
  stripe) - single carriageway
  (road with one lane on either
  side for traffic in both
  directions) = 60mph, dual
  carriageway (road with two
  lanes on either side for traffic
  in both directions) and
  motorway (road with four lanes
  on either side for traffic in both
  directions) = 70mph (going too
  slow or fast is a serious if

uncorrected quick enough, if
you miss a speed sign and go
too slow it will slow the flow of
traffic behind you and could
encourage them to overtake
you which could cause danger
but if you see the next speed
sign and speed up that could
only be a minor but going too
fast for more than about four
seconds will be a serious

- A blue speed sign means that is
  the minimum speed limit
- When it says slow in the road
  you must be going slower than
  the speed limit

Gap from car in front

- See when the car in front is at a
  certain point such as a sign or
  tree then count in seconds how

long it takes you to reach that point. Keep a two second gap from the car in front in dry conditions and four seconds if it's raining

- If a car pulls in front of you check center mirror and brake to restore the gap (can be a serious if fail to do it)

Zebra crossing

- Slow down even if no one is there but especially if someone is near the crossing because they might step out
- If the pavement at a zebra crossing is obstructed then slow right down and expect to

stop because someone could
step out last minute

Zebra crossing

Pedestrians

- Slow down when there are
  pedestrians on the pavement
- If a pedestrian is walking
  toward the road you wish to
  turn into and looks like they
  want to cross they have the
  right of way and you must wait
  for them to cross (treat it like a

zebra crossing so stay slow in case they just step out) (serious if don't wait) (however if the road you are turning into immediately has a pedestrian crossing with lights and the light is green then don't stop because the pedestrians have to wait for the lights to change to cross/ only stop if the light is red)

- Never wave someone on the pavement to cross the road because someone else might not stop (serious)
- When driving along if pedestrians are already in the road slow down and stop if necessary to let them cross

- However if pedestrians are in the middle of the road on the white line again do not wave them to cross on a dual carriageway, you can in the case it's a single carriageway and the car behind you has good distance to stop but it's not necessary to let them cross

Cyclists
- Hold back at safe distance and overtake when there is good observation of road ahead (apply signal)
- Never overtake on a bend or if there is oncoming traffic on a narrow road

Stop sign

- A junction that is harder than usual to see if something is coming
- The car must come to a complete stop before continuing (serious if fail to stop) (can put up handbrake to clearly demonstrate a full stop)

Stop sign (red)

Yellow box junction/ keep clear markings

- Can only go if the road you want to go onto is clear or you see there is enough room for your car

Yellow box junction

Junctions (instruction turn right)

- Look out for speed signs when approaching junctions that tell you the speed on the new road
- Center and right mirror

- Right signal

- Move into right lane if it's clear
(that's if there is a right lane if
not just continue in the lane
you're in)

- Approaching junction: apply
right signal (reapply if it
switches off – failing to do so
is a serious fault), slow down in
good time, and move into
second gear

- Rolling up to junction while
looking right and left (must
look left and right at least twice
even if it's clear – opposite
direction, your way, opposite
direction, your way, go) (failure
to check can be a serious so to
avoid confusion, fully/
obviously turn head and not

just look out of corners of eyes to clearly demonstrate to the examiner that you did check)

- At give way line (double broken lines) be positioned on the side you want to go; so if going right be on right side of the give way line at the junction (if was going left then be on the left side of the give way line facing in the left direction so not having to pull out then do a sharp 90 degree turn left instead it's like already going left with just slight adjustment (unless there is a cycle lane in which case never go in the cycle lane which can be a serious if there is a cyclist coming))

- If it's clear because there are no cars or there is a suitable gap

then go (check both ways twice
again before moving and look
in the direction of lower
visibility last because that is
direction where a car can
appear last second and poses
most potential danger)

- If still moving while
approaching the line and have
checked both ways twice and
have good visibility down the
road both ways and can see it's
clear then no need to stop at
the line, but if it's not clear or
you can't see down the road
both ways then stop at line and
go into first gear then when
there is a gap, or a car
signalling left coming from the
right side or there is a car

signalling right coming from the left side which will act as a block to oncoming traffic on the right when turning down the road you're on, then go if it's clear on the left (before going try to be certain there isn't a motorbike coming from the right behind the car that's turning as it might try and overtake the turning car and you will pull out in front of it) (failing to go when it's safe is a minor for hesitation but can be a serious if causing person behind to slow or holding people up (they might sound horn) and can be a serious also if miss multiple opportunities to go as people behind might try and overtake which can cause danger, it can also be a

serious if you pull out without
a suitable gap and make
someone have to brake)

- Once entered new road cancel
  signal if necessary and adjust
  speed

Give way sign and road markings

Roundabouts (instruction take 3rd exit)

- First exit is 9oclock, second
  exit is 12oclock, and third exit

is 3oclock. Taking an exit before and at 12oclock = left lane, after 12oclock = right lane

- As soon as getting the instruction or seeing a signpost saying third exit then check center and right mirror, apply right signal, and move into the right lane if clear
- Sometimes there can be two lanes that have a marking with a right arrow showing you can go right in both lanes so in this case always choose the left lane turning right but it's not serious if you don't see it and go in the right one
- Slow-down in good time as nearing and move into second gear

- Rolling up to roundabout while looking right
- If its clear (because either no cars or there is a car signalling left which will act as a block) then go (failing to go when safe is a minor for hesitation)
- If it's not clear stop at the line and go into first gear
- When clear check left mirror and pull onto roundabout and maintain good lane discipline - stay positioned in between the lines on the right-hand/ inner lane (if there were two right lanes then be in the lane before the outer-most right/ inner lane)
- Reapply right signal if necessary

- When just about to pass second exit check center and left mirrors then as soon as passed apply left signal then if clear merge into left lane and take the third exit

- If there are three lanes - once just about to pass the first exit check center and left mirrors and apply left signal and merge into the middle lane then once just about to pass second exit check center and left mirrors and reapply left signal if it's gone off and merge into left lane to take the third exit

- In event not safe to merge into a left lane apply right signal and go around the roundabout again and try again (there's no fault if don't manage to merge into left lane and go around

again but if try and go when
not safe it's a serious

- Once taken exit cancel signal
and look for a speed sign and
adjust speed and if not already
move into the left lane because
the right lane is only for
overtaking but because the
right lane is for overtaking you
have to be going the speed
limit otherwise cars will be
overtaking you on the left and
you won't get the opportunity
to move to the left lane but it is
serious if fail to do so

On the other hand if couldn't get
into right lane approaching
roundabout then you must take
the first or second exit (can't go
past 12oclock) - do not try and

get into the right lane when on the roundabout because you will cut someone up which is a serious and also do not try and just go around the roundabout in the left lane and take the third exit because the car in the right hand lane will be coming across into the left lane to take the third exit and will cut you up which will cause dangerous driving and is a serious fault so you have to take the first or second exit and come back around again (no fault for taking the wrong exit) - same procedure just if you're going to take the first exit apply left signal while approaching roundabout, if taking second exit (straight) then no left signal until just after passed first exit to avoid misleading cars waiting to emerge from the first exit because if they see you indicating left approaching the first exit they will think your turning into it and pull out in front of you and so this is a serious (sometimes the left lane might be left only (left arrow on road) in which case you have to go left and it's a serious if you don't go left)

Roundabout signs

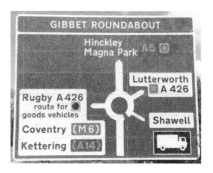

Mini roundabouts

You must give way to people coming from the right, so if you and someone on your right are pulling up to the roundabout at the same time you must let them go first

- Go left/ first exit - as approaching check center and left mirror then left signal, look right and if it's clear or there is a block (a car pulling off the roundabout and so blocking the other car on the right) then go, if not stop and go into first gear until clear
- Go straight/ second exit - as approaching check center and left mirror and no signal, look right and if it's clear or there is

a block then go, if not stop and go into go first gear until clear

- Go right/ third exit - as approaching check center and right mirror and right signal, look right and if it's clear or there is a block then go, if not stop and go into first gear until clear, once on the roundabout go slow and never go over the white circle and check center and left mirror before left signal to take the third exit

Mini roundabout sign (blue)

Motorways and carriageways

- As merging onto a motorway or carriageway in the merger lane have the right signal on and increase speed to match the speed limit of the motorway or carriageway and check your right mirror to assure it is safe to merge, check multiple times to assure there are no cars in your blind spot. If reach the end of the merger lane and it wasn't safe to merge then you have to stop and wait for a gap then once on quickly accelerate and increase gears to reach the speed limit

- You cannot overtake someone in a left lane. You can only overtake in a right lane

- As passing a merger lane if in the left lane if there is someone

trying to merge onto the
motorway or carriageway then
either slow down to let them
on, speed up to pass quick
enough so they can get on
without reaching the end of the
merger lane (don't exceed
speed limit), or move over to a
right lane then move back
when clear

Motorway sign (blue)

Forward bay parking

- Apply signal in direction toward the space
- Be on the opposite side/ as far away as you can from the space you intend to pull into
- When shoulder is in line with the middle of the space before the space you intend to pull into, dry steer completely in the direction of the space
- Creep forward slowly into the space
- If over steer stop, reverse, and then pull forward into the space
- If understeer it is too complicated to try and correct it and so it is best to reverse back to being in line with the space and start again

- Once in the space put the handbrake on and put the car in neutral

Reversing

- Steer left = back of car goes left
- Steer right = back of car goes right

Reverse bay parking

- Apply signal in direction toward the space (reapply it if it switches off at any point)
- Count three spaces in front of the space you are turning into and line up the middle of the front door window in line with

the third spaces first line/ the line closest to the space you are pulling into (every car might be a bit different so might require practice to figure out exact start position but it will typically be around the middle of the front door window)

- Put car in reverse and check over both shoulders and all mirrors
- Drive back slowly and immediately and sharply turn completely in the direction of the space you are going into (if not turning fast enough then before moving dry steer completely in the direction of the space then start reversing)
- Slowly let the car go back into the space, when in line with front of space/ you are facing

forward then stop and
straighten up

- If overturned and not straight
then look in mirrors to see
your position and go forward
to correct if necessary until
straight

- Reverse back straight into the
space until there is a small gap
between your spaces front line
and the bottom of the wing
mirror and put the handbrake
on and put the car in neutral

Parallel parking

- Apply signal in direction
toward the space (reapply it if it
switches off at any point)

- Pull up alongside the parked car about a meter or doors length width and so the back of your car is in line with the back or front of the car next to you depending on which side is facing the space
- Dry steer one full rotation of the wheel in the direction of the space you are pulling into
- Check over both shoulders and all mirrors – if someone is walking or there is a car do not move and wait for them to pass or signal for them to let you park before continuing (look over your shoulder on the side facing the road just before you start moving) (serious)
- While either looking over your shoulder out of the back

window or looking in the
center mirror, reverse slowly to
angle the back of the car
pointing into the space and
stop (this is where the front of
the car will swing out into the
road so again failure to check
down the road both ways
before moving will be a
serious)

- Dry steer back one full rotation
  to make the wheels straight
  again
- Check over both shoulders and
  all mirrors again and again wait
  for anyone to pass
- Reverse back slowly into the
  space but not too much and
  stop (if reverse back too much

you will hit the kerb which is a serious)

- Dry steer in the direction away from the kerb completely and look around again, then slowly reverse back into the space adjusting the steering if necessary to make sure the front of the car is not going to touch the car in front (if the space you are trying to get into is large then for the starting position you can have the back of your car further back behind the car next to you and this will make it easier when reversing into the space because you don't have to worry about the front of your car possibly touching the car next to you). Aiming for a drain length distance from the kerb

- If too close to kerb and suspect you will hit it then stop, repeat observations, and pull forward then repeat with more distance from the kerb

- Once in line with the kerb give a good distance from the car in front so you can easily pull out but not enough so someone can park in the gap and trap you in, and straighten up the wheel and put the handbrake on and put the car in neutral

Final takeaway

The point isn't to get to somewhere so no need to hurry. The examiner is most importantly looking for; highway code understanding, car control, and safety so double checking and not willing to take risks or chances which could endanger other people.

The examiner is taking you on a route that they are very familiar with and knows every driving scenario which in a test sense can be referred to as obstacles that are coming up and is specifically watching how you handle each obstacle (obstacle being everything mentioned in this book). When approaching an obstacle, overtly demonstrate the steps which avoids confusion with the examiner not being sure if you did understand the obstacle so they can mark the obstacle as understood, you can even talk out loud if it helps and will literally tell the examiner that you understand the steps.

Good YouTube channels

- Conquer driving
- DGN driving school
- Driving Crawley
- Clearview driving
- Advance driving school
- Driving TV
- Drive London
- Driving school TV

I watched many lessons and mock driving tests on high-speed using video speed controller extension for chrome browser to watch more videos in less time.

Tips from my first test (I passed on my second attempt)

I failed my first attempt due to a serious because the instruction was to go straight at the next roundabout so I approached in the left lane but then at the roundabout there was a left turn only mark on the road, there was no one around but I didn't have enough time to change into the right lane and while I was already in the go left lane the examiner repeated the instruction of go straight so I went straight - I should have went left then got told to come back.

The roundabout can be seen at the five-minute mark of Driving Crawley's Real Driving Test

Crawley Rush hour & raining!
CRAZY drivers in a rush?? video.
https://www.youtube.com/watch
?v=lpc3qVxLFJY

Another good resource for
questions if you don't already use
it is Googles AI chatbot Gemini

Google
https://gemini.google.com   ⋮

<u>Gemini - chat to supercharge your ideas</u>

Bard is now **Gemini**. Get help with writing, planning, learnir

Google

Sign in

Use your Google Account

Email or phone

Forgot email?

Hello again

Tell me what's on your mind or pick a suggestion.

Understand   Create

📍 are we there yet?   gaming podcast tag

🖼 (Enter a prompt here

Other books by Henry
Norsworthy

Direct Biology

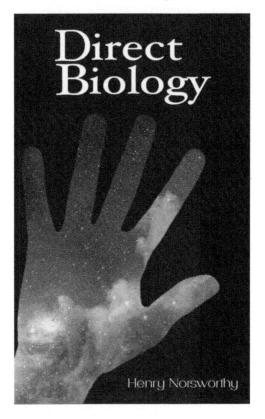

Change the past in the future –

a look into the existence of time

(Cover in process)

Toxin-Free Living in Modern Times

(Cover in process)

What I wrote to get an A* on the English Language GCSE

What I wrote to get an

A* on the

English Language GCSE

Printed in Great Britain
by Amazon